THE TRUE STORY OF
QUINTILIUS

Lois Szymanski

4880 Lower Valley Road • Atglen, PA 19310

DEDICATION

This book is dedicated to the memory of my twin,
Jim Knight, who left the world too soon.
Much love until I can hug you again.

Other Schiffer Books by the Author:

Chincoteague Ponies: Untold Tails, 978-0-7643-4085-7, $24.99
The True Story of Sea Feather, 978-0-7643-3609-6, $14.99
Out of the Sea, Today's Chincoteague Pony, 978-0-8703-3595-2, $14.95
Chincoteague Pony Identification Cards, 978-0-7643-4453-4, $19.99
The True Story of Miracle Man, 978-0-7643-4420-6, $14.99

Other Schiffer Books on Related Subjects:

Copyright © 2014 by Lois Szymanski

Library of Congress Control Number: 2014939563

Designed by Molly Shields
Type set in Cicero Caps/Avenir LT Std (TT)

ISBN: 978-0-7643-4709-2
Printed in China

Published by Schiffer Publishing, Ltd.
4880 Lower Valley Road
Atglen, PA 19310
Phone: (610) 593-1777; Fax: (610) 593-2002
E-mail: Info@schifferbooks.com

For our complete selection of fine books on this and related subjects, please visit our website at www.schifferbooks.com. You may also write for a free catalog.

This book may be purchased from the publisher. Please try your bookstore first.

We are always looking for people to write books on new and related subjects. If you have an idea for a book, please contact us at proposals@schifferbooks.com.

Schiffer Publishing's titles are available at special discounts for bulk purchases for sales promotions or premiums. Special editions, including personalized covers, corporate imprints, and excerpts can be created in large quantities for special needs. For more information, contact the publisher.

CHAPTER ONE

Keymar, Maryland

Golden fingers of evening sunlight stretched through the door, striping the floor of Chester's stall as Caroline pitched the last forkful of dirty straw into a wheelbarrow. The thick chestnut pinto stuck his head in the door from the outside, took a step forward, and nudged Caroline as if to say, *Hurry up! Let's play!*

"I'm finishing up now," she told her boy, a smile playing at the corners of her mouth.

The Chincoteague Pony stood very still, his ears twitching back and forth as if he understood. In many ways the pair did understand each other. They'd been best friends for the past three years, ever since two women from the Feather Fund had delivered the two-year-old pony to Caroline's family farm, unloading the gelding from the trailer and handing over the lead rope.

It was warm for an early March day in Maryland. Caroline pushed the wheelbarrow out of the barn and dumped it on the muck pile. Then she wheeled it into the tack room and grabbed a lead rope from a hook.

A few years earlier, Caroline had sent an essay and application to a nonprofit group called the Feather Fund. She prayed she'd be picked by the Feather Fund to win a Chincoteague Pony foal, but she'd been disappointed to come in second place. Then, a few months later the phone call came from the Feather Fund. Caroline remembered waiting while her mom talked.

"The Feather Fund placed a foal in a home two years ago and the girl no longer wants the pony," her mom explained after she'd hung up. "You're the next in line. Do you want him, Caroline?"

And so the pony came to her. She named him Chincoteague Treasure Chest and called him Chester. He was gentle and kind and easy to train.

"Come on, boy," said Caroline. "Let's go." She shook away memories and smiled at her pony. Then she grabbed a bridle from the hook just around the corner. He held his head down for her to slide the bridle over his head. She buckled it tight and slid onboard. Chester was easy enough to ride without a saddle, and so today she rode bareback. Within moments they were riding through the large pasture by the lane, sweeping along at a choppy trot. She leaned forward and cued him to canter.

The pinto extended his stride effortlessly. Caroline's long blonde hair blew out behind her, the cool evening air burned her cheeks, and at that moment she felt she was one with the pony, one with the world, one with the universe. The blurry landscape passing by slowed as Chester's pace dropped to a trot, and then a walk. She reached down to pat his neck. "My boy," she whispered.

"Nice pony."

Caroline spun around. She'd been so into her moment with Chester that she hadn't seen the woman walking on the road on the other side of the fence. She recognized the neighbor who lived a half mile up the road and smiled. "Thanks."

"Your legs are awfully long. Isn't he small for you?"

Caroline swallowed a hard lump. The exhilaration she'd felt moments ago faded fast.

"He's a little short, but he's stocky," she said, her heart pounding. "He has no problem carrying me."

"Oh." A gust of wind swirled up the road, and the woman pulled her jacket zipper up to her chin. "I just wondered."

Caroline watched the woman's back as she walked away.

She hated that her day had been spoiled. She knew she was a little lanky for her pony, but why did the neighbor have to point it out to her, especially when she was feeling so good?

Chester was easy enough to ride without a saddle, and so Caroline rode bare-back. Photo by Lindsey Markle.

"If I saved enough money could I buy a bigger Chincoteague Pony?" She asked it without thinking, although Caroline guessed it had been in the back of her mind for a while.

"Why not get a local horse?"

"I like this breed, Mom," Caroline said. "They are healthy and smart and easy to train. Some of the mares have foals that reach horse size. And, anyway, I never did get to go to the island." She thought about reading *Misty of Chincoteague* and of how much she wanted to see Chincoteague and Assateague islands and maybe even see Chester's sire, Witch Doctor. Chester's dam, Duchess, had already passed.

Caroline followed her mom into the kitchen and Pearl trailed her, tagging Caroline's ankles with her snout, looking for another scratch. Caroline plopped into a kitchen chair, reaching down to scrub fingers across Pearl's raised head.

Dishes clanked as Mom put away plates and spoons, cups and silverware from the dishwasher. "You'd have to ask your dad," she said, "but if you earn the money yourself, I don't see why not."

The problem was, when Chester stopped growing, Caroline did not. Now five-foot eight-inches tall, her legs dangled when she rode, especially bareback like today. If only he'd been bigger, like some of the Chincoteague Ponies she'd seen in photos online. Some grew to horse size, but Chester was only 13.2 hands, a little on the small side.

"Come on Chester," she said, turning the fuzzy pinto. "You're perfect the way you are, and we are fine together. We're not going to let anyone ruin our day."

Saying it didn't make it so, though. No matter how much she tried, Caroline couldn't shake the shadow that one careless sentence had cast over her day.

That night, after dinner and homework, Caroline sat on the sofa petting her pot-bellied pig, Pearl. She scratched the black swine behind her ears, and popped the question to her mom.

That night, Caroline got her laptop out and logged onto Facebook to see if anyone had posted new photos. Foals at the Pony Penning auction often sold for thousands of dollars. Caroline wondered if she really could save enough money on her own. She stared at the screen. Someone had posted a photo of Witch Doctor. He was a thick stallion, like his son Chester, and they were marked the same, too, except Witch Doctor was a black and white pinto.

Caroline imagined what it would be like to bring a wild foal home and train it up on her own. She sighed and closed the laptop. She knew it would be hard to earn enough money on her own, but there was only one way to find out. She had to give it a shot.

CHAPTER TWO

Assateague, Virginia

The bay mare, Mermaid, trailed her leader, Witch Doctor, toward the trees in the distance. Two chestnut mares and a foal tagged behind them, forming a line that stretched along the shoreline. Wild Island Orchid was in the middle with her newborn pinto foal and Rap the Wind brought up the tail. The five of them trudged on, the breeze lifting mist from the water and spraying their faces as they followed the line of the bay.

They were a small but tight herd. On this day, they grazed along marshy edges of the bay, working their way across the north end of the Virginia side of Assateague Island. They picked their way through the shallow waters of high tide to look for tender shoots.

The wind picked up, whipping Witch Doctor's forelock back and blowing his long mane out like a flag in the wind. The weather was changing, as it did frequently on Assateague Island.

Witch Doctor was a wise old stallion with years of experience. He protected his mares with his heart, and right now, he could feel a storm brewing. It was time to take his mares into the trees for shelter.

Witch Doctor lowered his head to nuzzle Mermaid. They talked for a moment in grumbles and tiny nickers. Then he gave her a push with his muzzle. The mare knew what he wanted, and she turned toward the pine forest.

Witch Doctor circled his mares, urging the three of them forward. The chestnut pinto foal scampered alongside his mama, all legs and whiskers. The old stallion had rounded his girls to bring up the rear. They picked up their pace, heading for the forest, cool blue water stretching out behind them. Mermaid and Rap the Wind were round and full with foal. Soon, all three of his mares would have foals at their sides, a sure sign of the warm weather to come.

Witch Doctor was a wise old stallion with years of experience. Photo by Linda Insley.

CHAPTER THREE

April 14, Lancaster, Pennsylvania

The sun made a valiant effort to pierce rays through the early morning fog, but the haze was so thick that windshield wipers and headlights barely cleared a path to see the road ahead. Caroline leaned her head against the cool window pane, lulled by the hum of wheels. They followed a line of rugby team cars led by Coach Brad, heading for a match in Lancaster, Pennsylvania. To Caroline, it was the most important match of the year.

The rugby team was psyched. They had to win this match against Hempfield, one of their biggest rivals. Today they were playing in honor of Rita, a teammate who had been killed in a car accident earlier that year.

Caroline looked down at the pink shoelaces woven through her cleats in Rita's memory. The team had chosen pink because it was Rita's favorite color. She closed her eyes and remembered how Rita had always been the first to comfort others. Once, on the flight home from a match in Utah, the turbulence was bad and the ride became very bumpy. Most of the team was terrified, but Chardonnae had freaked out. It was Rita who held Chardonnae's hand the entire way home, burying her own fear to comfort someone else.

Caroline recalled the texts she once got from Rita, random notes that said, "Hey, love you, girl!" Now she was gone. There were no more texts from Rita. They had to win this match. It was the least they could do to honor her.

The ride was long, and Caroline dozed. The next thing she knew, Rachel was shaking her. "Wake up, Caroline. We're here," she said.

Caroline groaned and piled out of the car behind her friend. She shook off the sleep. Almost immediately she felt herself pumping up for the game. She loved rugby. It bred infectious energy and was the only game with the grace of soccer, the speed of track, and the power of hockey all rolled into one.

Soon they were preparing to kick off the ball. On the sidelines she heard the sounds of children playing, interspersed with tweeting birds. The sun wrapped its warmth around her, removing the chill. A ball thumped. The official blew his whistle, and the first kick sailed through the air. The idyllic morning was about to get rough.

Pink laces turned brown with mud as the line of defense drove back attack after attack, cleats tearing up once-green turf. The score shifted back and forth, with the team barely holding onto the lead. Then they were down to the last thirty seconds of game. That's when Caroline's luck turned south.

A girl from Hempfield had broken through the line of defense. She came at Caroline, a mass of anger with cleats. Caroline's heart banged in her chest as the nearly six-foot-tall girl pounded toward her.

The team jokingly called this girl Yeti, but that moment Caroline understood the power and talent heading right for her. In that moment, Yeti seemed almost as broad as she was high. Caroline momentarily cringed and then slowed, crouching to prepare for the tackle.

She'd been through hundreds of tackles just like this one, but this time something felt different to Caroline. She knew it was going to be bad. She stretched out her arms, reaching to wrap like any successful tackle, but the hit was a hard one. When the two went down, Caroline's left leg was caught in the tangle. She felt something pop as the full weight of Yeti descended.

There was a snap and another pop. Caroline's kneecap slid north. Pain ripped through her leg, flashing from knee to thigh like lightning.

A whistle blew, slicing the crisp air.

Pink laces soon turned brown with mud as the line of defense drove back attack after attack, cleats tearing up once-green turf. Photo by Yvonne Gamble.

Yeti rolled from Caroline and then stood, stepping on the leg that already grinded with pain. Caroline yelped, and was immediately surrounded by scouts and officials. She tried to lie still but couldn't. The pain was too great. She rolled in agony. Strong hands reached to pin her to the ground. The official's face blurred.

Caroline took a deep breath and remembered what she had to prove and who this game was for. She took another steady breath.

"Can you stand?"

The coach's face wavered above her. Dizzily, she nodded. "I think."

He took her hand and helped her to her feet. The crowd erupted into cheers and applause. Embarrassment slid over her. "I'm okay," she said.

"I'll be the judge of that," Coach Brad said. He threw an arm over her shoulder and helped her to the sideline.

"I can do this, Coach," Caroline pleaded. "Put me back in the game."

The trainer sat her down on the bench and manipulated the leg. "It feels a little loose," he said, his brow furrowed.

"I'm fine," Caroline pleaded. "Let me play and I'll have it looked at tomorrow."

The trainer looked at the coach and shrugged as if to say he wasn't sure.

Coach Brad sighed. "Listen, Butler. We don't know how bad that leg is injured."

"Come on, Coach." She stood up and put all her weight on the leg and then took a few steps. "Look at me. It's fine now. I just had the snot knocked out of me."

Coach Brad considered her words. "Let's test it," he said. "Run out about twenty yards."

Caroline jogged forward. Pain shot through her leg, but she put on a game face. She was tough. She could do this. She turned to jog back toward him.

"Back pedal," Coach Brad shouted.

Caroline threw it in reverse, jogging backward.

"Okay, cut to the right."

Caroline felt shaky. She cut to the right.

Cut left!"

She stretched her step and cut left. A powerful snap rang out, and she went down, mid-stride. Caroline sucked in a sharp breath and watched her leg flail out in an unnatural position. Horror filled her. She shrieked in pain. Before Coach Brad could reach her, she was sobbing.

She was out of the game and knowing that filled her with emotions that were almost as powerful as the initial pain. Anger filled her. That Yeti! Grrrr… There was humiliation. She felt ashamed she wouldn't be able to finish this game that meant so much to her. Not just to her, but to the entire team.

"She needs an ambulance," the trainer said, and Coach Brad nodded.

"No!" Tears streamed down Caroline's face. Her knee was already almost the size of her thigh, but she would not leave the game. She had to be there, even if it only meant cheering her team on. She had to be there for Rita.

"Let me stay. It can wait," she said, her hand on the swelling knee. "Please. For Rita." Tears streamed. The coach looked her full in the face, and then slowly nodded.

Caroline's friend Tulia was in the game. Her mom, Ms. Taborga, made her way over to sit beside Caroline on the bench. "If you want me to take you home, we can skip the after-game celebration and leave as soon as it's over," she said. She handed her phone to Caroline. "Call your mom and tell her what's going on and let her know that I'll be driving you home."

Caroline nodded.

CHAPTER FOUR

Assateague, Virginia

Witch Doctor looked massive when he pulled himself to attention, like now. He let out a deep whinny, a bugle call to his mares. Mermaid nipped at the other two, herding them back. As lead mare, it was her job to follow his commands, and just now he was telling her to keep the herd at bay. She didn't wonder why because she could see Phantom Mist trotting toward them.

The shimmering chestnut stallion had already lifted two mares from other herds. Now his target was Witch Doctor. If he won the battle between the two of them, he would win Witch Doctor's mares.

Phantom Mist pranced forward, tossing his head and stretching long forelegs out in a show of power. Mermaid stood at a distance, watching with the other mares and the young filly. She remembered how Witch Doctor had plucked her away from Sockett to Me's herd in a massive battle of teeth and hooves. At twenty-five years of age, Witch Doctor was not as fit as the younger stallions, but he had skills they had not yet mastered.

Now the two stallions faced each other. They turned in a parallel prance, a dance of sorts that stallions often do before battle. They trotted side by side, tossing heads until

The two stallions, Phantom Mist and Witch Doctor, faced each other. Witch Doctor was the first to rise up on hind legs. Photo by Sydney Tytler.

manes ruffled and tails billowed like flags. Each one assessed the other before they turned to face off again.

Witch Doctor was the first to rise up on hind legs. As she watched, Mermaid realized this old stallion had thick muscles, worn by age but bulging just the same. He rippled in the sun, and hairs in his thick black mane stood on end, his hooves pawing the air.

Phantom Mist rose high in a face off. Black hooves raked the air in a show of power until they both came down with thuds. Dust rose. Witch Doctor whirled to kick. Mermaid heard the thunk of hoof on hide and the squeal of anger that followed. On a dime, Phantom Mist spun and shot toward Witch Doctor, mouth open.

For a moment, the two were a whirlwind of teeth and hooves, and then the chestnut was trotting off, his body a sheen of sweat and sun. He whinnied to his waiting mares. They whirled to join him and the herd left the service road, galloping into a sea of green, causing a flock of white egrets to rise into the air, flapping their protests.

As Witch Doctor moved toward them, Mermaid saw the gash in his shoulder. She realized Phantom Mist's teeth had taken a small chunk out of her stallion, and she moved closer to nuzzle him. Witch Doctor touched her nose, and the two of them huffed and grunted.

Orchid and Rap the Wind had already moved away from them, grazing without care. The new filly had flopped down in a sunny patch and now dozed in the warm, soft pasture. Witch Doctor returned to grazing. Mermaid gazed into the distance, trancelike. She watched the sleeping foal flip his fuzzy tail at a horse fly, and she longed for her own foal to arrive.

CHAPTER FIVE

Maryland

It was late when Mrs. Taborga pulled into the Butlers' driveway. Caroline's mom was waiting. She thanked Mrs. Taborga and hugged Caroline as soon as she saw her, but then her eyes dropped to the knee. She saw the size of it, and her face grew somber.

"The doctor's office won't be open this late, so it's either the ER or the Urgent Care Center," she said, her voice grim as she helped Caroline from Mrs. Taborga's van into the family truck.

On the drive to the Urgent Care Center, Mom asked Caroline about the accident and Caroline filled her in, sharing every detail. Mom reached over the console and took her daughter's hand. "Whatever happens, it will be okay," she said.

When she saw Caroline limp in, leaning heavily on her mom, the receptionist at the Urgent Care center brought a wheelchair.

The wait seemed like forever, even though the place was empty. Caroline zoomed around the room in the wheelchair. "I could get used to this," she joked. "Wheelchair races!"

Mom frowned. "It's not going to come to that," she said, and Caroline sobered. She hoped her mom was right.

After an X-ray, the doctor came to take a look and to speak with them. He carefully unwrapped the bandage. The knee had inflated to the size of a football. When he pushed on the swollen knee, concern filled his eyes.

"It looks like something is torn in there for sure," he said. "It's too swollen to get the full picture, but this is definitely not a regular boo-boo. I think we are looking at a serious injury."

Caroline's stomach rolled over.

He patted her good leg. "Don't get upset until we know more," he said, but his voice sounded like a rehearsed speech.

The nurse slipped into the room with the X-rays. The doctor placed them on a white light board to study. Caroline tried to read his face, but it was blank.

Finally, he turned away from the light board. "Maybe I was wrong," he said, but his voice sounded doubtful. "I can't find anything out of place on the X-ray. Perhaps it is just a bad sprain."

A smile started in Caroline's heart and rose to her lips.

"I'm writing a prescription for Naproxin to help with the pain, and here's an order for an MRI." He handed over the two papers and bent to scribble in his folder. "No school until we get the results of the MRI," he added. "Keep it elevated, and use the crutches."

The next week was a whirlwind of doctor appointments, first with the specialist and then for the MRI. It took two days for the results to come back. Caroline passed the time propped up on the sofa, logged into Facebook perusing photos of the ponies on Assateague. A huge group of online friends were Chincoteague Pony fanatics, too, and they had begun to post pictures of the first foals of spring.

Caroline scrolled through the Pony Ladies page. There was Kachina's foal, a big solid palomino that everyone was already in love with. Poco Latte's black-and-white pinto was another favorite. Babe had a solid bay colt, just like the one she'd had the year before. That one had been placed with Amy, a Feather Fund winner. Lyra's Vega had a pretty chestnut filly, and there was a blurry photo of Wild Orchid and her foal. Beside them were Rap the Wind and Mermaid, both of them looking as if they were about to bust. Caroline thought about her dream. She wondered if she could really save enough money by summer.

Caroline propped her leg up on the arm of the sofa. Coach Brad was on the phone. The team had qualified for

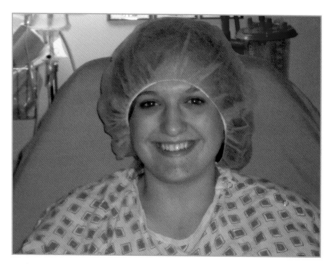

Before her knee surgery, Caroline smiled to ease her mom's mind. Photo by Karen Butler.

muscle connecting the calf to the back of your knee. Every ligament and tendon in the knee has been torn. The medial and lateral meniscus are shredded. You're looking at total knee reconstruction."

Caroline felt tears sting at the back of her eyes and she let them come. What about California? Worry ate at her. She'd never had surgery. What if it didn't go right?

"So I won't be able to finish the school year?"

Dad shook his head, no, and Caroline hung her head. Her thoughts were all over the place, and she felt dizzy. *While the team heads off to California for the national championship, I'll be sitting at home,* she thought. No horseback riding, no hiking, no fun! She bit her lip and blinked back tears. Why did this have to happen to me?

April 24, 2012 Westminster, Maryland

Caroline's mom pulled the sheet up to her daughter's chin. "You'll be fine," she said, but Caroline noticed how Mom could not sit down, how she kept busy picking at the covers and patting Caroline's leg, but not looking her in the eye. Caroline smiled to ease her mom's mind.

The doctor had explained everything earlier, showing Caroline a picture of the knee. They were going to graft the patellar tendon and drill a hole through the knee to screw it in. Everything would be held together with a pin, but then she'd have months of physical therapy ahead of her.

The nurse soon wheeled her up to surgery. Without Mom or Dad, real fear began to set in.

"Are you okay, honey?" the nurse asked.

Caroline nodded but her heart was pounding.

The doctor leaned in, lifting the thin white blanket to give her a shot. "This will relax you," he said, and Caroline forced a smile.

The nurse hooked a mask over Caroline's ears and settled it over her mouth. Her eyes grew heavy and she began to dream. She and her mom were making a recipe they'd seen on the television last week, one that looked so good. It was macaroni and cheese with crab meat and Old Bay Seasoning sprinkled throughout. And then she slept.

nationals again, and this time they'd be going to California. "If my knee is only sprained, I might be well in time to play," Caroline said excitedly.

"That would be good," the coach answered.

"I've never flown all the way across the United States, so that would be cool," Caroline added.

"If you listen to everything your doctor says maybe you'll be able to…"

Caroline didn't hear the rest of Coach's answer. Her parents had come into the living room, and the look on their faces told her something was very wrong.

"I gotta go, Coach. My parents are home with my medical results. I'll call you," Caroline said. She hung up, her mind whirling. How bad could it be?

"We're sorry," Mom said.

Caroline's mind scrambled. "Why? What did you find out?"

Mom closed her eyes. "It's really bad," she said. Her voice cracked. She sat down beside her daughter. "It's everything. You tore everything in your knee," she said.

Caroline felt her world begin to shift. She took the paper from Mom's hand. Everything was garbled and written in technical language. Her heartbeat increased as confusion and frustration slipped in. "I don't even know what this means," she said, crumbling the paper in anger.

Dad grimaced. "You tore your ACL and your MCL," he said. "You shredded your medial meniscus and tore the

CHAPTER SIX

April 24, 2012   Assateague, Virginia

The sun drifted lazily between the clouds on this spring afternoon. Mermaid stood basking in the sunshine in the patchy grass meadow. There were three herds in the big meadow, clustered in groups. While the others grazed on salty marsh cord grass just beginning to green, Mermaid stretched her head long and low and closed her eyes, soaking up the warmth. The foal inside her had been still throughout the night, settling deep. The mare knew he would arrive soon.

Witch Doctor raised his head and watched the mare stand in contemplative silence. She'd moved away from the rest of the herd. The black-and-white pinto stallion had been around long enough to know that Mermaid's time was coming soon. Even though she'd been with the younger stallion Socket To Me in the spring, and Witch Doctor knew the foal was not his, the stallion's protective instincts kicked in. She was his mare now. He would protect her at all costs.

Rap the Wind and Orchid buried their noses in waving meadow grasses. The sweet smell of spring shoots had drawn them to the marshy meadow, and their stallion had not resisted. Birds were singing, the sun was shining, and signs of new life were all around.

Witch Doctor moved away from Mermaid, stepping between the two mares and lowering his head to graze. He sensed that Mermaid would head into the trees soon to have her foal alone. That was the wild pony way. The older stallion would give her the privacy she needed while watching over the remaining herd. He'd keep Rap the Wind and Orchid on this side of the meadow until the new foal arrived, yet stay close enough to be there for Mermaid if needed. In less than a month, the third foal would arrive and he'd have a full herd again.

Mermaid watched Witch Doctor rest his nose on Orchid's back, and she sighed. Her stomach contracted. It was time. She stepped toward the smell of pine, slipping between the hardwood trees and the loblollies, searching for a soft place to deliver her foal.

The colt arrived in the dark of night, sliding from his momma in a rush. Wet and weak, he quivered when the night breeze ran its brush across his back, painting him with life. He was a big one, with four long white stockings and a star on his forehead. Chestnut markings covered a sparkling white body. White patches were decorated with tiny light brown dots and the big white marking that saddled his back and spread around his belly was balanced by a large chestnut circle in the middle.

Mermaid stood up as soon as he was born. She nuzzled the colt, grunting and nickering while checking every inch of him. He was perfect. She raked his wet coat with a rough tongue and whinnied softly, letting him know that he was her own.

The colt's ears drooped, but as the mare groomed him and the blood flowed through his body, they perked up, two fuzzy points. He scrambled to stand, sliding and falling into the sandy bed of pine needles. He stretched out his front legs and hoisted again, slipping and going down.

Mermaid stood close, urging him to try again. She nickered and he answered—a throaty little greeting that filled her heart. He pushed himself up once more, and then he was standing, a strapping big colt beside his big bay dam.

Mermaid touched her nose to his, ran it down his legs, and then placed her nose gently on his back. She would give him a moment and then urge him forward. Instinct pushed her to get back to the herd. Pride urged her to introduce her new boy to the world.

The newborn foal emerged from the trees with his mother, lowering his head to stare at the two mares and the thick black-and-white stallion. Photo by Kathleen Cahall.

By the time they emerged from the trees, the colt was trotting shakily, but he slammed to a stop when he saw the others. Witch Doctor rumbled a greeting, and the colt's ears flew up and then flickered back and forth. He lowered his head and stared at the two mares and the thick black-and-white stallion.

Mermaid gave the colt a soft shove and nickered, telling him it was okay, so the colt followed when she strode past him. He watched the stallion touch noses with his mama, but then he saw something far more interesting. There was a foal his size with two mares, just past the stallion. He nickered joyously, and the filly came running.

CHAPTER SEVEN

Maryland

Hazy. Everything blurred. The clock slid back and forth on the wall. Caroline blinked, trying to clear the haze. Dad's face was leaning over her. "Hey there," he said.

Then Mom's face came into view. "Welcome back," she said. "The doctor said you did just fine."

Caroline swallowed a scratchy lump in her throat. Groggy at first, now she felt like she was going to throw up. She gagged, and the nurse handed her mom a container, just in case, but she was okay.

"Here, swallow a little ginger ale. That will help," her mom said. The nurse handed her mom crackers, too, but Caroline was too groggy to eat anything.

It was late afternoon, almost evening, before the hospital cleared Caroline to go home. The doctor said her heartrate had gone up during surgery and they thought she was going to wake up, so they'd given her more anesthesia. That had made it harder for her to wake up.

At home, Caroline opened the car door and swung her legs out onto the ground. She pulled herself up and tried to take a step on the bad leg. She lurched forward.

"Whoa there," Dad said, grabbing her by the back of the shirt. "You just had surgery. You can't walk on that leg." With Mom on one side and Dad on the other, they helped her into the house.

Once in bed, Caroline slept again. Over the next few days she fell into a pattern of watching television in bed or sitting with her laptop, cruising through the foal photos now being posted on Facebook almost daily. Other Feather Fund kids logged in regularly, and Caroline found herself chatting with them online. This year, the Feather Fund would be helping Alana in New Hampshire and Mollie in Massachusetts purchase foals at the 2012 Pony Penning auction. Caroline began to watch their online discussions. If she was lucky enough to get a foal, Caroline didn't want to choose one that a Feather Fund kid wanted.

Two weeks after surgery Caroline was able to use her crutches. She slowly hobbled to the barn. Even though she was still getting used to the crutches, she was able to get the gate open and slip inside the fence. Bending, she turned over a water bucket to sit on and settled outside the stall doors, watching the ponies in the distance. Chester and the old miniature horse grazed side by side.

The sun was out, and it was warm for an early May afternoon. Caroline closed her eyes, and let the rays warm her. Less than a moment later, she heard pounding hooves. Chester had spotted her and now he came running, sliding to a stop to nuzzle her hand, looking for a treat.

"I don't have anything for you, boy," she said. The touch of his muzzle on her hand was like magic, filling her up, healing her soul. He lowered his head. She tussled his forelock and rubbed the whirl of hair on his forehead, and by the time she picked up her crutches to go inside, she'd found a new determination. She would bring home a friend for Chester, no matter what it took.

That evening Caroline cruised the Facebook pages of all her Chincoteague Pony friends. She searched for new foal photos while Mom sorted through jewelry.

"Alana said this bay pinto colt is her favorite," she said, turning the laptop for her mom to see. "It's Leah's Bayside Angel's colt."

Mom looked at the photo. "He looks big," she said.

"Yep, he'll be big," Caroline said. "His sire is Leonard's Stud."

Jewelry clinked as Mom put two necklaces on hooks. "Do you really want to buy a foal this year?"

Caroline nodded. "And I think Lois will have room for me in the Feather Fund house."

Chester stopped grazing when he saw Caroline was back at the barn after her surgery. He came running to nuzzle her. Photo by Lois Szymanski.

"Will she take you along?" Mom asked.

Caroline clicked to go to her favorite page. "I think so," she said.

There was a new album with photos of Witch Doctor's herd on the *I Love Chincoteague Ponies* page.

"Hey, Mom, someone found Witch Doctor on the north end." She hurried to click on the album. Witch Doctor was Chester's dad, and she wouldn't miss a chance to see him.

The first photo showed the black-and-white stallion strolling along the park road. "If Chester was black, he'd look just like his sire," she told her mom. "They're marked the same."

She stopped cold at the second photo. "Oh my gosh!" she squealed. "He has two foals and both of them are chestnut pintos!"

Mom moved to look over her shoulder. "That's a blurry photo," she said.

"Yes, but they're Chester's half-siblings! It says the one on the left is a colt. The other one is a filly. And Mermaid's colt will be big because she's one of the biggest mares on the island!"

Caroline peered at the colt as her mom moved back to the jewelry box. He was taller than the filly, with a star on his forehead, stockings on the forelegs that came to just below the knee, and rear stockings that stretched above. He was tall and leggy and his markings were perfect.

"Mom," Caroline said, her heart full and her voice almost a whisper. "I think I found my colt."

CHAPTER EIGHT

Late May on Assateague Island, Virginia

The foal leaned against his momma and watched a bus ambling up the service road. His ears perked up, and he flared tiny pink nostrils when the smell of rising dust floated across the meadow.

Mermaid lowered her head into the tall cord grasses. She was used to the appearance of the bus. It brought people with cameras and binoculars. They came to look for the ponies. They came to photograph the many varieties of waterfowl and bird life. They came to see endangered species like eagles and Delmarva fox squirrels. They watched egrets high-step through the waters and ospreys dive to spear fish in the bay, but they never bothered the ponies or the wildlife.

Mermaid took two steps, and then looked back at her colt. He was a leggy one and would become a tall boy one day. He'd grown a lot over the weeks. As she watched, he took off, trotting forward a piece to see the bus and causing Orchid's foal to stir from an afternoon nap.

Moments later, two foals were ripping around the pasture, bucking and kicking, stopping to sniff noses and then taking off again.

Mermaid watched. She'd been through many summers and many foals. She loved the warm, sunny days before Pony Penning came, but she also knew what Pony Penning meant, and she didn't like it. She knew that was the week when time with her foal ended.

Pony Penning always unfolded in the same way. First the cowboys came to round up all the bands. Then, early on a Monday, the northern bands were herded down the beach. As the morning sun rose, casting warm rays across a rippling sea of blues and golds, the northern bands were brought down the beach and on to the southern pens. There, they joined the bands of ponies who lived on the south end of the island.

Mermaid watched her foal take off, trotting forward a piece to see the tourist bus on Assateague Island. Photo by Kathleen Cahall.

Once they were in the southern pens, people would come in droves to see the ponies. Some foals would be tagged as Buy Backs, foals that would go to auction to be sold, but with the understanding that the pony would go back to the island to live forever to help replenish the herd.

On Wednesday, the saltwater cowboys would herd all the ponies into the bay to swim to Chincoteague Island for the auction. Thousands of spectators would come to watch the wild ponies swim.

Mermaid could feel Witch Doctor watching her, but she didn't turn to him. She continued to stare toward the bus, so lost in thought that she didn't even see it disappear into the foliage at the turn. She didn't see egrets rising into the air to make a flag of shimmering white or the cruise boat rounding the bend out on the bay. In her mind, she saw Pony Penning week.

Mermaid knew she had a limited number of days left to be with her colt. On Thursday, after the swim, all the foals not tagged to go back to the island would be sold at the auction on Chincoteague Island.

Mermaid nudged her colt close and then buried her head in the grass. She tore off a giant squeaking mouthful. Maybe they would choose her son for a Buy Back this year, just as they had a few years back. Maybe she wouldn't lose this one. Maybe he would stay.

CHAPTER NINE

Keymar, Maryland

Caroline stayed up late that night, messaging people on the Pony Ladies page. She wanted to know more about the colt, and she wanted to know which ones the Feather Fund kids had picked out. The last thing she wanted to do was to bid against them and the Feather Fund. After all, they'd given her Chester.

She noticed she had a Facebook message from one of the ladies. She read, "That's not Witch Doctor's foal. She was with Sockett to Me last year, so that would be his colt."

Caroline's swallowed. So he wouldn't be Chester's brother, but Sockett was a tall stallion and that meant the colt would be even bigger. He been born in Witch Doctor's herd and nurtured by Witch Doctor, so that had to count for something, she told herself.

After turning off the computer, she quickly fell asleep. The pain in her knee had quieted, and she was beat.

The sun crept under the curtains and across the floor boards. Weak rays of early morning light stealthily slipped into Caroline's bedroom. She rolled onto her side in bed, blinking and playing over in her mind the dream she'd had, seeing the image of the foal she'd nearly touched. She'd been on Assateague. Even though it was a place she'd never seen before, the image was still alive and real in her mind's eye.

She slipped out of bed and turned on her computer. Had anyone seen Mermaid's elusive foal in the past few days? She decided to do a quick check for Facebook messages, and she had to make a plan. She had ideas of how she could add to her savings and that meant a talk with Mom. Maybe she could sell her motorbike. That would add at least $700 to her funds. And her brother had asked her if she wanted to take over his job mowing the cemetery weekly. Her heart beat excitedly. Bad knee or not, she was going to say yes.

Caroline's mind was still buzzing when she saw the post on Alana's page. Alana had posted the same photo of the two foals Caroline had seen the day before. Under it, she wrote, "Mermaid's foal is my second pick."

The Feather Fund would set a dollar limit. If the first pick foal went too high, Alana would have to bid on her second pick.

Caroline's heart plummeted. She was filled with a restless urge. She had to think. She had to be with Chester. He would set her mind straight, and the mindless chore of mucking stalls would help, too.

Chester came running when he saw Caroline. He stopped to watch her pick the stall. He moved forward, his warm nostrils whuffing at the back of her neck. She stopped to scratch his head, but her mind was not with him. Mermaid's foal had wormed his way into her heart.

She leaned on the rake and scratched Chester's head under the thick forelock. "He could become your best friend," she told the chestnut pinto. He comes from your world."

I have to bring that colt home, she thought. But there were so many "what ifs" that could stand in the way. What if she couldn't save enough money? What if Lois couldn't take her along to Chincoteague for Pony Penning? What if Alana didn't get her first pick?

Mom popped her head into the stall. "You're not overdoing it, are you?" she asked.

Caroline stuck her leg out to show her mom the brace was in place. "I'm fine," she said, her voice steady.

Mom's eyes met Caroline's. "What's wrong?"

Unexpected tears welled up. "Mermaid's foal is Alana's second pick!" she blurted out. "I'm in love with that colt, Mom. But what if I don't get to go? What if I can't save enough? What if Alana doesn't get her first pick and decides to bid on my boy?"

Worried that she might not get the new foal of her dreams, Caroline went out to the barn to ease her mind. Chester came running when he saw her. Photo by Caroline Butler.

Mom stepped into the stall, resting her hand on Chester's rump, her eyes full on her daughter. "It's too early to worry about so many things," she said. "Get your father's blessing, first. Then, talk to Lois and see what she says and we'll see how much you can save. One step at a time."

Caroline sighed. "I guess you're right."

Mom put her arm on Caroline's shoulder. "Sometimes you have to count on things to unfold the way they are supposed to."

She knew her mom was right.

After dinner, Caroline headed downstairs to the family room. Dad was watching sports, Pearl stretched out on the sofa beside him, snoring softly. Caroline sank into a chair, waiting for a commercial.

"Dad," she said at the first break. "I have to ask you something."

He looked up. "Okay, shoot."

"I've been saving money for a while, and I'm going to start mowing grass at the cemetery for more money and I plan on selling my motorbike…"

He raised his eyes expectantly.

"I really want to buy another Chincoteague Pony. If I come up with the money on my own, would that be okay?"

Dad paused. "You have a Chincoteague Pony."

"I've grown five inches since Chester arrived!" Caroline's words rushed out. "I've picked out a foal that's going to get big, maybe even close to 15 hands, but he's going to cost at least $1,000, so I want to sell my motorbike to add to my savings.

Dad looked exasperated. "You could get a registered quarter horse for that."

She sighed. "I don't want a quarter horse. Everyone has quarter horses. Chincoteague Ponies are different, Dad. Look at Chester. He's practically bomb proof. Look at how he carried that calf out of the ravine without blinking an eye. He's an asset to this farm." She paused.

"That's how Chincoteague Ponies are," she continued quietly. "I love Chester and that's why I want another one, a bigger one."

The game was back on. Dad sighed, a half smile playing across his lips. "If you can save the money and you have a way down and back I guess that'd be okay."

Caroline's heart did a backflip. She hopped up and crossed the room to hug her dad. One step closer, she thought. One step at a time.

CHAPTER TEN

A red vehicle cruised along the service road, moving slowly, men inside watching. Mermaid knew the vehicle carried saltwater cowboys checking on the herds, noting where to find them, getting ready for the impending roundup. Photo by Captain Debbie Ritter.

June on Assateague Island, Virginia

The field on the right side of the service road was full of ponies. Mermaid raised her nose, breathing in the scent of Sockett to Me, Spirit, and other ponies she knew. A late-night rain had moistened the salty cord grasses, drawing many to the meadow to graze.

A red vehicle cruised along the service road, moving slowly, men inside watching. Mermaid felt the weight of midsummer upon her. She knew that vehicle carried saltwater cowboys checking on the herds, noting where to find them, getting ready for the impending roundup.

Witch Doctor's head flew up.

In the distance, Spirit was approaching. Witch Doctor spun to nip at Mermaid. In turn, she wheeled around to nip Orchid and Rap the Wind. The mares pushed the foals to follow.

With the his herd safely away, Witch Doctor drew himself up to full size, turning sideways, facing the chestnut roan pinto trotting toward him.

Spirit was a Maryland stallion who had come south to Virginia years ago. He'd jumped the barrier that separated the state herds. The Chincoteague firemen returned him to Maryland—only to find him back again a week later. They returned him once more, but the stocky pinto had his eyes on a bay mare on the Virginia side, and he wasn't about to give up. The third time he leaped the barrier, officials in Maryland told the firemen to keep him. The stallion already named Spirit of Assateague by Maryland officials became a Virginia resident just as he wanted, but he got a new name in the process. The firemen called him Yankee Spirit.

Now, Spirit slid to a stop and gazed at the mares who had moved away. He glanced back at his own mares in the distance and seemed to have second thoughts. He snaked his head from side to side and then whirled, returning to his herd.

With the danger averted, Witch Doctor trotted to his mares. He nosed each one gently and grunted his approval. With just one more glance at Spirit and his herd, they all lowered their noses, back to the business of grazing.

CHAPTER ELEVEN

Keymar, Maryland

The next day, Caroline talked to her brother, Tommy. She could start mowing the cemetery at the Middleburg United Methodist Church, he said, and it was just up the road, close enough to walk.

"It pays $75 per cut," she told Mom as they rode into town to shop. "Do you think I could get $800 for my motorbike?"

Mom nodded. "I'll put an ad in the paper for you tomorrow morning," she said.

Caroline jumped when her cell phone rang. Glancing at it, she smiled. "That's Lindsey," she said. "I gotta get this. She was going to check to see if they need more help at Middlefield Farm, the barn where she works."

A moment later Caroline was glowing. "I got the job," she said.

Mom wrinkled her brow, her lips turned down. "I don't want you to overdo it," she said. "If you mess up that knee, you'll be looking at another surgery."

"I won't. I promise," Caroline said. "It's not like running or walking too much or doing jumping jacks." She laughed. "And I'll have the brace on. All the stress will go to my back."

Mom made a face, but followed with a smile. "You could put some things in my booth at the antique mall, too," she added.

Caroline grinned. "Great idea," she said, thinking of all the trinkets she'd picked up over the years. Her room was full of odds and ends she'd taken a liking too, but none of them were as important as getting a colt—Mermaid's colt.

That evening, while Mom cooked dinner, Caroline boxed up items: An old painting a neighbor had given her in exchange for help cleaning, an antique jewelry box, a stack of old books…. Every little sale would add to the stash growing inside her dresser drawer.

After dinner, Caroline logged onto Facebook, looking for more pictures of Mermaid and her colt. The big bony bay was an elusive mare, though, and not many photos had been captured. Caroline clicked on the message box to compose a note to Lois with the Feather Fund.

"Do you have room for me in the Feather Fund house?" she wrote.

An answer came quickly. "Yes, we have room for one more. We split the cost by the number of people in the house so the expense is less than $200 a person for the full week."

"If I go, do you think I could ride with you?"

"Sure. I'd love to have you along, Caroline."

The week flew by, and then the next. There was mowing and mucking and then the call from her mom while she was out with friends. "Someone wants to buy your motorbike for $700? Is that okay?"

Yes, yes, yes, it was okay. Seven hundred dollars more!

Three days later, Caroline got her first check from Middlefield Farms. She'd worked nearly every day for the past two weeks and now her reward was big, over $400. She added it to the rest. Now she had $1,100 stacked neatly inside her dresser drawer. But how much more would she need?

Three times a week, Caroline rode with her mom into town for physical therapy at Central Maryland Rehab. At first, she couldn't even push the pedals all the way around on the exercise bike, so they'd added hip exercises. Now, even though there were occasional popping sounds, she could pedal a bike. They moved her to the weight room to do leg presses and had her running on an underwater treadmill. At home she did squats to build muscle and walked all the way to the ravine to check on cows with her mom several

Even with physical therapy sessions three times a week and the new jobs she took on to raise money for a new foal, Caroline found time for her beloved Chester. Photo by Karen Butler.

times a week. She was up to 200 pounds on the leg presses, but at night her leg throbbed. Still, she found time for her beloved Chester.

One night, just home from physical therapy, her leg was filled with shooting pains. She walked to the barn. It was a warm clear night, and the sky was full of stars. She plunked down on a bench outside Chester's stall door. Staring up at the stars she pictured Mermaid's colt. Over the weeks her heart had wrapped itself around the big chestnut pinto. She didn't know what she would do if she couldn't bring him home with her in July.

The sound of crunching gravel made her look up. A shadow moved down the driveway and to the pasture gate. The gate creaked open and shut.

Mom smiled and sat beside her on the bench. "You okay?"

"Sure. My leg was hurting some, and I needed to be outside," Caroline said. She tilted her head skyward. "I can't stop thinking about my colt."

Mom joined her in staring at the stars. "Do you remember the story the minister shared at Christmas this year, the story of the first star?"

Caroline nodded and closed her eyes to remember. In the story, Quintilius was the Christmas Star chosen to shine over baby Jesus when he was born.

"The star was called Quintilius." Mom echoed Caroline's memory. "I think that would be a great name for a colt," Mom said quietly.

Caroline rolled the name over in her mind. It was perfect.

CHAPTER TWELVE

Early July on Assateague Island, Virginia

Mermaid's colt leaned into her side, his head turned toward Chincoteague, watching a line of men on horseback plod along the service road. Their voices cut through the morning mist.

Mermaid watched Witch Doctor. He'd frozen, head held high to watch the men.

These older horses knew what it meant when saltwater cowboys rode up the service road. Some of them looked forward to it. Once they were penned, people would come to gaze at them with love in their eyes. They would be given yummy hay and troughs full of cool, fresh water. Even swimming the bay was okay. They did it all the time on their own anyway, paddling over to Pope Island to find fresh grass and sometimes even swimming to Chincoteague in the dark of a full moon night to steal sweet shoots of corn from the farmers' fields, swimming back again before the sun rose. The only bad part was losing their foals.

The mares turned, following Witch Doctor down the hill to the water's edge. It was a hot day. The waters of the bay invited them, cool blue and barely moving. Mermaid moved into the water and Quint followed, testing the cool liquid with tiny steps. They moved along leisurely, leaving the cowboys behind.

Later in the afternoon, the herd moved up the hill a piece, into the cool pine trees. Mermaid rested her head on her young son's back. She breathed in the warm, sweet smell of him. She closed her eyes and savored the moment. Soon, he could be gone.

Mermaid moved into the water and her foal followed, testing the cool liquid with tiny steps. Photo by Kathleen Cahall.

CHAPTER THIRTEEN

Chincoteague and Assateague islands, Virginia

For Caroline, the ride to Chincoteague seemed to take forever. Lois's car was small. There wasn't much room to stretch her bad leg out. By the time they stopped in Cambridge for gas and coffee, her knee was throbbing.

Caroline tested her leg gingerly before walking inside the mini mart, and when they returned to the car, she reached into the back to get the thick black brace she was supposed to wear. She wrapped it around her leg.

"You better keep that on," Lois said.

"It drives me nuts," Caroline said, smiling wryly. "But I will."

"Have you ever been to Chincoteague?"

"Nope," Caroline replied. Her heart pounded in anticipation. If only they could fly. She'd read *Misty of Chincoteague* and other Chincoteague Pony books and she'd dreamed of wild Assateague Island. She pictured Chincoteague Island as a quaint little fishing town with tiny corrals for ponies and fishing boats docked on the bay.

"Can you believe this year is the eighty-seventh swim?" Lois said. "They've been herding the wild ponies up, having them swim across the bay and auctioning off the foals for eighty-seven years now. It boggles my mind."

Caroline smiled. Eighty-seven was a lot of years. She could picture the islands in her mind, and she wanted to see them. She wanted to see where Chester was born. And she couldn't wait to see Quintilius.

It might not be good that I've already named Quintilius, Caroline thought. *It'll hurt a lot more if I don't get him, now that he has a name.* But then she switched gears, swearing in her mind that she *would* get him, no matter what happened.

"I saved $1,500," Caroline said, thinking of the last dollars she'd added to her stack of saved bills. "Do you think it will be enough?"

"You never know," Lois said. "Some go very high, but last year a few went for under a thousand dollars. I have a feeling it'll be enough."

Caroline settled back in her seat. "I hope so," she said. "I already have a name for him," she added," and then she launched into the story of why she'd named him Quintilius.

As Lois drove, the pair chatted about ponies and the island and foals they couldn't wait to see and how Caroline would finally get to meet some of the other Feather Fund kids. She'd been chatting with them online now for over a year, and they already seemed like friends. The miles zipped by and at last they were crossing the causeway, the long and winding bridge onto the island.

There was Chincoteague off in the distance. It was noon and the sun was high. The water shimmered, looking like a thousand diamonds atop blue, glinting where the sun hit and bounced rays back. The shoreline was a mix of new hotels and old docks, with fishing boats and colorful crepe myrtles blossoming along the shoreline.

As they drew closer, there were stakes where oyster beds were marked off. Billboards lined the causeway. "Visit the Chincoteague Pony Center," one said. "Chincoteague Pony Farm—Foals for sale," another one declared. There were ads for restaurants and hotels, too.

Fishermen glided by on small boats and big riggers passed, headed out to sea. There was even a Coast Guard boat sliding by with men in uniform lining the deck. Caroline shaded her eyes when Lois pointed out the Coast Guard station on the right side of the island.

"Does it look like the place you imagined," she asked, and Caroline nodded.

"Exactly," she said. She was surprisingly calm, even though her heartbeat had picked up.

The late-afternoon sun was shining on the tall red-and-white striped lighthouse that symbolized Chincoteague and Assateague islands. Photo by Lois Szymanski.

"After we grab a bite and drop our stuff at the house, what is the first thing you want to do?"

"I can't wait to see Assateague and to find Quint." Caroline stirred in her seat. They were over the bridge and stopped at the red light that brought them onto the island.

"This road is the main drag to Assateague Island," Lois said, pointing straight ahead at Maddox Blvd. "The old bridge used to come in by the firehouse and you had to turn left to get to Maddox, but this new bridge changed everything."

Caroline nodded. She'd seen photos of the old bridge.

"After we get lunch we'll head over to Assateague Island. Since it's a wildlife refuge we'll have to have a pass for the week."

By the time the pair had checked into the house and Caroline had met her roommate, Lindsey, and the other volunteers staying in the house, it was late. They'd missed the roundup of the southern herds, but they decided to head across the bridge to see the south herd in the pens.

The late afternoon sun was shining on the tall red-and-white striped lighthouse that symbolized Chincoteague and Assateague islands. Caroline stared at it. She wanted to pinch herself. Was she really here, in the place of her dreams?

A family had gathered on the bulkhead below the bridge to Assateague Island—a mom, a dad, and two boys. A bushel basket sat beside them. They dropped strings into the bay, bait tied onto the ends, and waited to net a crab.

"They're crabbing," Lois said. "We used to do that with our kids when they were little."

Caroline nodded. She couldn't' think about crabbing when ponies filled her head. She looked down at the list of foals on the notepad in her lap. Her second pick was in the southern herd, a chestnut filly with a teardrop-shaped marking on her forehead. The filly's sire was Surfer Dude, a well-known southern stallion with mustang in his breeding.

Caroline didn't have to look at her list. She had her favorites memorized, but she scanned the list just the same. Her third pick was also on the south side of the island, a chestnut colt out of Tuleta Star. The colt had a big round diamond on his forehead and was most likely out of the chestnut pinto stallion, Courtney's Boy, but neither would compare to Mermaid's foal. She closed the notebook. Quintilius had to come home with her. He just had to.

The lady at the toll booth smiled. Lois paid and put the pass in the car's windshield. The road unfolded ahead of them, with trails marked and bikers passing by. They passed the trail to the lighthouse on the right and the Herbert H. Bateman Center on the left.

"We'll stop there tomorrow," Lois said, pointing to the nature center. They have some cool exhibits, photos, art work, and a bunch of good books."

The car rolled around another curve. They were heading toward the ocean. Caroline could smell it in the air. Tall pine trees mixed with shrubs and hardwood trees, and in between it all there were myrtle bushes. On the left, water stretched out, blue and full of life. Tall white egrets dipped beaks into the water while ducks and geese floated lazily. Black Cormorants dove under the water, surfacing seconds later. The water became a canal.

"Are we close?"

Lois pointed ahead. Cars lined the edge of the road. "All those cars are parked because everyone is here to see the ponies at the pens."

They slid into a parking spot. Caroline grabbed her camera. Lois pulled out a can of mosquito spray. "We need to spray each other first," she said, smiling. "The mosquitos are so big here they should be the state bird."

The ponies inside the pens had separated into bands with each stallion commandeering the movement of his mares and foals.

"There's Miracle Man," Lois said excitedly. "Isn't he gorgeous?"

Caroline looked at the bay-and-white pinto with spattered dots surrounding larger brown markings. He held his head high, a thick mane cresting his neck, a coal black forelock covering his forehead. He was handsome.

"Miracle Man was an orphan near death when he was found on the island. It's a miracle he lived," Lois said. "I always look for him. He tends to throw smaller-sized foals, but I love him to pieces."

They leaned on the fence to watch the ponies. Lois said when the herds came together at the water tanks, sparks could fly, but that didn't happen today. Only the foals showed spark, racing around each other, their mothers and the other mares, playing tag in the pens.

"Hey, there's Lyra's foal!" Caroline said, spying her second-choice pony. "She's beautiful!" The tall chestnut filly was even prettier than her photos had showed. "But what's that red tag on her neck?"

"Uh, oh! She's a Buy Back," Lois said.

"So she'll come back to the island for the rest of her life, right?"

"Yep. I'm sorry."

"It's okay," Caroline said, "but Mermaid's won't be a Buy Back, right?" Lois had already told her the fire company probably wouldn't keep any colts. She said they already had enough stallions on the island. But Caroline wanted to hear her say it again.

"I hope not," Lois said. "They have a lot of young stallions coming up. I can't imagine them keeping another."

Caroline nodded and scanned the herd. There was Tuleta Star's foal in the far corner with Courtney's Boy's herd. He was smaller than he'd looked in her photos, pretty, but not really what Caroline was looking for.

She closed her eyes for a moment, her heart beating madly. A sudden longing came over her. It was okay that Lyra's foal was a Buy Back because only one colt mattered. She hoped she had enough money to make him hers.

CHAPTER FOURTEEN

Late July on Assateague Island, Virginia

Loud whistles and the shouts of men on horseback roused Mermaid from her rest. She'd been dosing on her feet while her colt slept in the lush grass beneath her. But now she was suddenly wide awake. It was here. The day she knew was coming.

When the cowboys approached, Witch Doctor stamped his hoof, but stood very still, his head over the backs of his mares. He knew he had to go, and he wasn't about to run.

He left running to the young stallions who thought they could escape. Witch Doctor was too old for that silliness. He knew the drill.

Two cowboys came toward them, their horses at a lazy trot. The one with a full gray beard sat high on tall chestnut. A younger cowboy on a stocky dark bay followed, his red ball cap shading his eyes but not the smile that played across his lips.

The roundup began. In the distance, other bands of ponies were being approached by different sets of cowboys. They would all merge together when they got to the pens. Photo by Stacey Steinberg.

Witch Doctor pushed the mares forward and they headed toward the pens just up the service road. The cowboys didn't have to tell them where to go. Witch Doctor had been through this enough times to know, but the two pinto foals had not. They rolled their eyes and whinnied in fear, high-pitched nickers that rang out, echoing across the marshlands.

In the distance, other bands of ponies were being approached by different sets of cowboys. They would all merge together when they got to the pens. It was one of the few times each year when they had to be near each other and had to get along.

Mermaid knew the younger stallions would fight in the pens. She thought of her foal and how she would have to keep him close, away from the ruckus of young stallions butting heads. There would be sweet hay in the pens and full tubs of fresh cold water, water without salt tinging its flavor. She looked forward to that.

The cowboys were talking to each other as they trotted along. Mermaid remembered the older, more seasoned cowboy. He had rubbed his hands down her neck in the pen at the last roundup, his voice soft and full of admiration. He'd had a blue, checked shirt on that day, and he wore the same one today. She trusted him.

The gates to the pen were just ahead. As they approached, a big man swung the gate wide open. Witch Doctor slid over beside his mares, boxing the foals in between him and them, and they passed through the gates into the pen. The cowboys swerved away, outside the pen.

Mermaid lowered her nose to her colt, touching his back as they moved forward to the back of the pen, letting him know she was there and they would be just fine. Pony Penning had arrived.

CHAPTER FIFTEEN

Chicoteague and Assateague islands, Virginia

Caroline spent most of Sunday hanging at the southern pens, taking photos and meeting friends she'd known online for what seemed like forever. They all loved these ponies as she did, and many were Feather Fund kids, like Alana, who would see her dream come true at the auction on Wednesday.

"I actually won *last* year," Alana told Caroline. "But then my Dad got laid off, and my parents thought it was best to wait another year."

"Bummer," Caroline said. "That had to be awful. How'd you handle that?"

"I cried a lot," Alana answered. "I hung out all week last year with Lindsay. Have you met her?"

"Not yet," Caroline said and then smiled. "I'm rooming with Lindsey Scott. She volunteers every year, but I haven't met Lindsay Geiser yet."

"Boy was it hard watching Lindsay get her foal last year. And then Amy was awarded the bay yearling that the fire

Caroline and her Feather Fund friend Alana watched the bay pinto colt Alana wanted to buy and name Spartan. Photo by Lois Szymanski.

company donated to the Feather Fund, and to top it off some ladies came begging the Feather Fund to help another girl who kept getting outbid, and they did. It was really good stuff, but it was hard for me. I'm just glad the Feather Fund bumped me up as an automatic 2012 winner."

"Me, too," Caroline said.

"See that dark bay pinto colt?" Alana pointed across the pens to the tallest foal in the pack. "That's Leah's Bayside Miracle's colt."

Caroline nodded. She knew from their chats online that Alana had fallen for the colt, but he had a serious roman nose and didn't look attractive at all to Caroline. At least he was a big one. "I hope you get him."

"And I hope you get Mermaid's!" They both turned back to the pens, resting their arms on the top fence rail.

"Tomorrow you'll finally see your boy," Alana said. "Are you going to the beach run to see them bring the north herds down?"

"Yeah, Summer said she'd pick me up," Caroline said, referring to another Feather Fund kid. She ran a hand over her face. "It's killing me that I haven't seen him yet."

"I bet."

"We'll both get our colts. At least I hope," Caroline said. She let out a heavy breath. "It's too much to worry about it," she added, but even as the words left her mouth she felt the familiar gurgle of apprehension turn over in her tummy. "It's gonna stink if we don't get them."

"Yeah," Alana agreed. "Seriously."

On Monday, Caroline's alarm rang out at 5 a.m. She scrambled from bed.

Lindsey was already awake and dressed. "Summer's picking us up in fifteen minutes!"

"Ugh." Caroline could hardly get the grunt of acknowledgement out. It was too early for pleasantries but she didn't want to miss the beach run and a chance to get her first glance at Quint.

She could picture it, the cowboys bringing the northern herds down the beach against the backdrop of the majestic Atlantic Ocean. She splashed water on her face. *I might get photos of him*, she thought and her heart beat faster. By the time she came out of the bathroom five minutes later, she was fully dressed, wide awake, and ready to go. After all, her new baby was out there.

CHAPTER SIXTEEN

Late July on Assateague Island, Virginia

"Ayeeee! Hup, hup, hup there!"

Mermaid bolted forward when the cowboy's voice rang out. She followed Witch Doctor and Orchid. They all knew where they were going.

Mounted cowboys on all sides whooped and hollered as the string of ponies headed east toward the ocean, turning when they hit the sand to head south.

The sun had barely crested the dark ocean. Tentative rays stretched out, bronzing purple blue waves with warmth.

It felt good to trot along the ocean while the sun was low and the breeze whipped back her mane and forelock, but Mermaid still felt low. Each step she took south was one step closer to the time when her foal would leave her side forever.

Mounted cowboys on all sides whooped and hollered as the string of ponies headed east toward the ocean, turning when they hit the sand to head south. Photo by Brenda Boonie.

CHAPTER SEVENTEEN

Chicoteague and Assateague islands, Virginia

The crowd cheered when the first cowboy came into site. The sun was just up, a big golden ball that cast warm rays over the white-crested ocean waves. Caroline felt its warmth roll over her shoulders as she watched a string of ponies come into view behind the saltwater cowboy.

The ponies trotted along, manes and tails billowing out behind them, many with foals at their sides, some whinnying for foals who had gotten behind or in front. Caroline raised her camera to snap a few pictures of their approach. The deep rumble of a mare calling out was quickly echoed by the weak and quivery returning nicker of a young foal.

Veronica and her friend, Jerry, and Summer stood with Lindsey and Caroline, close to the red ribbon boundaries refuge managers had strung on stakes to keep the crowds back. The ponies came closer, and then they were streaming past. Caroline was torn between raising her camera to snap photos and keeping it down so she could look for her boy without a viewfinder in the way.

"There's Mermaid," Veronica said, elbowing Caroline.

Caroline's eyes settled on the colt. He held his head high, eyes rolled back, little nostrils flaring as he lifted his front legs like high-rising pistons and pressed against his momma's side. As she watched, the crowd disappeared. It was just her and the foal and the big bay mare… Perfection passing by.

And then he was gone, lost in a sea of ponies heading toward the beach road and inland to the south pens.

Caroline joined the throng of people heading for their cars and for the pens. Veronica, Jerry, Summer, and Lindsey and Summer's friend, Michaelanne, were all chatting and giggling as they walked, but Caroline dropped back, quiet. She'd finally laid her eyes on the boy she wanted to take home and now that want became a need, a need so deep inside that her heartrate had picked up and her stomach was doing flip-flops. Would she have enough money… and what if she didn't?

Caroline didn't fall sleep until late that night. After an entire afternoon watching her boy at the pens, her determination was solid. He would go home with her.

The sun glared down, Caroline leaned on the weathered fence board and gazed out over the ponies, looking for Mermaid.

A lot more ponies lived on the north end of the island. Now that they'd arrived, the pens were packed. The south herds had been relegated to the smaller pen on the right. The north herds filled the left pen. They clustered together in tight groups making it hard to see around one to view another.

Caroline had jumped at the opportunity when Lois asked if she wanted to join friends Syd and Sarah in helping fireman Dean and his wife, Laurie, with tagging ponies. They wanted help identifying the mares, and Caroline had been studying them online for quite some time. That's where she'd come to know Syd and Sarah—from those online connections.

A flash of black and white caught her eye and there was Witch Doctor, challenging Leonard's Stud through the fence. Then he pushed his mares to the far corner of the pen. She saw the tall bay to the left of him, and just ahead of her was Quint. The colt stood apart from his momma, peering through the fence rails, that distinctive white star on his forehead shining white.

A smile spread over her face. He was exactly what Caroline dreamed of.

Sarah nudged her. "He looks great," she said.

Caroline nodded.

"You'll get him," Syd said when she saw the worry etched on Caroline's forehead.

A flash of black and white caught Caroline's eye and there was Witch Doctor, challenging Leonard's Stud through the fence. Photo by Stacey Steinberg.

The late July sun beat down on the cowboys as they pushed the first mares through the shoot. Beads of sweat rolled down Caroline's back, and she twisted her ponytail into a makeshift bun.

Each foal scampered after its momma into the shoot where it was stopped and tagged. The foals fought back, rearing and bucking when they were grabbed. Less than a moment later, they were released wearing a new sort of necklace, a string with a tag that bore their number.

Each time a foal came through the shoot, the girls called out its dam's name, and Laurie wrote it in her book next to the assigned number.

As soon as Mermaid exited the shoot the firemen grabbed Quint. Caroline called out "Mermaid" before the firemen even had the tag on his neck. Laurie smiled because she knew he was Caroline's favorite. The colt was tall with a refined head and nostrils that flared wide. He raised his head and let out a high-pitched whinny, quivering anxiously.

Caroline's heart beat fast. She wanted to touch him, but she knew the rules. The girls weren't allowed in the pens and they'd been told not to touch any ponies.

Dean tied a tag around Quint's neck with the number 42. As soon as he released the chestnut checkered colt, he flew to Mermaid's side, snorting and slamming to a stop beside her. All three girls giggled.

Caroline saw sweat running down Dean's face. He swiped it away as he helped two more cowboys herd a new mare into the shoot, followed by a buckskin stallion named Copper.

"Run 'em through," the cowboy named Kenny called. "She doesn't have a foal, and he's stuck to her like glue."

"E.T.," Syd said, and Sarah nodded. The mare might have been a bay pinto but her head was as Arabian as could be. She arched her neck and held her head high and proud. She was the stallion Copper's only mare and he wasn't letting her go.

Caroline stared at the mare. Her body was round with foal.

"I bet she won't give birth until fall," Sarah said.

"She's got a ways to go," Caroline agreed.

Caroline watched Copper and E.T. join Witch Doctor and his mares at the water troughs, dipping noses deep into the cool water. The older stallions seemed to have an understanding. They didn't tramp around the pens looking for a fight like some of the younger stallions who were snorting and challenging everything in sight. They simply eyed each other and stuck close to their mares.

"I love Witch Doctor," Caroline said.

"Me, too," Syd said.

Sarah nodded. "Copper, too."

"Girls!"

Oops, a foal's in the shoot, Caroline realized. "Rambling Ruby," she called, naming the dam.

"Yep, and that's a Spirit baby," Syd agreed.

The sun grew hotter, and the afternoon wore on. By the time they finished and left the pens, Caroline was mopping sweat from her neck. Her pants and shirt were stuck fast to her, and she felt like she'd just finished up a rough summer rugby game.

CHAPTER EIGHTEEN

Pony Penning Week on Assateague Island, Virginia

Mermaid gazed across the pen. A tall girl with long blonde hair leaned on the fence looking their way. She'd noticed the girl on beach run day, had felt her eyes on them, and here she was again. There was something about the girl and the way she looked at the colt that reminded Mermaid of her own feelings. If she had to lose her boy, maybe he could go home with this girl.

Witch Doctor raised his head, ears alert. Sockett to Me approached. Mermaid looked at the stallion who'd once held her heart, but her loyalty was with Witch Doctor now. She watched as Witch Doctor rose on his hind legs pawing the air and snorting. That's all it took for the younger stallion to back off and return to his mares.

Mermaid munched hay, Quint at her side. People edged the pens, hanging on the fences, snapping pictures, shading their eyes against the afternoon sun. They raced closer to take photos of Sockett to Me challenging Witch Doctor, then retreated again. They followed the frolicking foals with their cameras. Each one looked different to Mermaid. There was the lady with the wide-brimmed sun hat and the bright pink shirt, the children who ran pointing from foal to foal, older men leaning on canes and holding purses for the women, firemen running fresh water into the troughs and spreading hay in the pens, and even a wheelchair parked at the far corner with a boy who had a camera of his own. It was the same every year, but this year Mermaid was scanning with extra interest. *Which of these people would take her foal home? Would they care for him? Would they love him the way she did, with all of the heart?*

Mermaid followed Witch Doctor to the water trough, her colt scampering behind. The trough was next to the fence where the tall girl with long blonde hair stood. As she watched, her colt dipped his head in the trough, snorting and blowing bubbles. He tossed his head, spraying the girl on the fence with water. She laughed and smiled at him.

"Oh, Quintilius," the girl said. "You are so cute." She raised her camera to snap a photo.

Mermaid moved closer, lifting her head from the trough, staring at the girl.

"You have a handsome son, Mermaid," the girl said softly. "Good job."

Mermaid contemplated the girl and then nickered softly.

"If I get the chance to take your boy home I will take good care of him, Mermaid. I'll love him like you do. I promise."

Mermaid munched hay, Quint at her side. Photo by Kathleen Cahall.

CHAPTER NINETEEN

Chincoteague and Assateauge islands, Virginia

Lois had just come into the Chincoteague house from her book signing at the Kite Koop when Caroline's phone rang.

"Hey, how'd it go at the pens?"

Caroline grinned. "Good," she answered, reaching for her phone. She scrolled down to read the text. As she read, her face grew hot and the room began to spin. She sank onto the living room couch. "Noooo. No, no!" She felt hot tears rising behind her lids.

"What?"

"It's from Alana," Caroline blurted. She tried to focus on the blurry text, took a deep breath, and then read the text out loud, voice quivering. "I'm at the pens and they are tagging Buy Backs."

She swallowed, her voice breaking. "They just put a red tag on Mermaid's colt."

"What?" Lois' face paled.

"You told me they wouldn't tag a colt!" Caroline blurted, accusation in her tone.

"I'm so sorry. Is Alana sure it's your boy?" Lois sat down on the sofa.

"Yes! She knows who he is!"

"I can't believe they would keep another colt. There are too many stallions on the island as it is," Lois said. "And they already have a full brother to that colt! Poseidon's Fury is out of Mermaid, by Sockett to Me. Why would they keep two stallions with the same bloodlines?"

"I don't know, but they are." Anger crawled up Caroline's spine. Lois had given her false hope. Everyone had misled her. They said the fire company wouldn't keep a colt this year, only fillies. Now tears erupted and rolled down her face.

"I can't believe it," Lois kept saying, over and over. "I bet they don't even know they have a stallion with the same bloodlines. I...."

Caroline stood up. "It doesn't matter. None of it matters," she said, walking down the hall and into her bedroom. As soon as the door slammed shut, her tears came in full force. She jabbed at numbers on her phone. She had to talk to Mom. Maybe Mom would come. Maybe they could just go home.

Caroline came out of the room at dinnertime on Tuesday. She knew her eyes were red, but she didn't care. Mom had said she'd leave to drive down in the morning, but even that was too long to wait. Right now she needed her more than anything.

Everyone in the house kept saying how sorry they were, but words like that didn't help. Caroline ate one piece of chicken and then went back to her room. Lindsey didn't follow. Caroline supposed she didn't know what to say, but there was nothing anyone could say anyway. Her dream had slipped away, and she had no one to blame except that simple red tag.

That evening, Caroline went with Lois and Lindsey to the pens. It was better than sitting in the house all alone and, truthfully, she had to see the tag for herself...just in case they were wrong.

She quickly found him in the pens. Quint stood quietly, his head dipped low, watching the crowds while staying close to his mama. Even from across the way Caroline could see the red tag that poked out from under his chin.

Alana was further down the fence with Molly, who would be getting a foal this year. They were both watching the bay pinto colt Alana wanted to buy and name Spartan. Alana turned and then saw Caroline. The pair walked down the fence line to chat.

Caroline pointed at Spartan. "I hope you get him," she said.

Quint stood quietly, his head dipped low, watching the crowds while staying close to his mama. Even from across the way, Caroline could see the red Buy Back tag that poked out from under his chin. Photo by Kathleen Cahall.

"Thanks," Alana said. "I am sorry about your pick."

Caroline nodded and changed the subject. "Do you have a favorite?" she asked Molly.

Molly nodded, blue eyes as bright as the smile she flashed. "Summer Breeze's filly. I love her so much!"

Caroline couldn't help but smile. "You'll get her," she predicted.

A moment later, Sarah sidled up next to Caroline as she propped her bad leg up on the bottom fence rail.

"When they tagged him, they were chasing a pinto filly," Sarah said. "When she got away they grabbed him instead. I really think they grabbed the wrong foal."

"Maybe when they realize he's a colt they'll take the tag off," Alana suggested.

Caroline shrugged. She didn't trust herself to talk, but she hoped they were right.

"We're going to tell Dean when we see him," Syd said, "just in case they think they tagged a filly."

Caroline turned to Lois. "Do you think they made a mistake?"

"I honestly don't know, Caroline," the older woman replied. "It sounds like they could have. I still can't imagine why they would keep him. Dean doesn't make those selections, though. I think Harry does."

"Do you know him?" Alana asked. "Could you talk to him?"

"I don't know him well enough to ask," Lois said. She hesitated. "We just have to respect their decisions," she added.

Caroline grunted. At that moment she couldn't respect anything. She wanted Lois or *someone* to do something to make that red tag come off her boy. She wanted to scream, she wanted to cry, and she wanted to go home. *I wish I'd never looked at all those photos of spring foals*, she thought. If she hadn't found him online she wouldn't have fallen in love with Mermaid's foal.

"Hey, over here," Alana shouted, waving her arm at two girls walking toward them from the road. "There's Veronica and Jerry."

Caroline watched them approach.

"I'm sorry about Mermaid's colt," Veronica said.

"Yeah, me, too," Jerry echoed. "I thought they'd realize they made a mistake and take the tag off."

"Me, too," Caroline said. She felt heat rise over her face.

"Are you going to the swim in the morning?" Sarah asked.

"We are," Alana said of herself and her family. "How about you, Caroline?"

"Lois said she's not. She says it's too crowded for her, but I'd like to go. I've never seen it."

"We usually come over here to see them leave the pens, instead of going to the swim," Syd told Caroline. "Then we go to the beach. It's the emptiest day of the year. Everyone is at the swim so we get the beach to ourselves. Do you want to go with us?"

Caroline didn't even know if she wanted to see the swim now that Quint had been stolen away. The invitation to see them leave the pens sounded good. "Yeah, I'd like that," she said.

"Do you think you'll bid on another one," Syd asked softly.

Caroline thought about Lyra's Vega and her beautiful chestnut colt with the red tag around his neck, too. Things just weren't meant to be, she guessed. "Nope."

"Wasn't Tuleta's foal your third pick?" Alana asked.

Caroline turned away, gazing out over the ponies.

Witch Doctor rested his nose on Mermaid's back. She was dosing, one rear hoof resting while Quint nursed. "I'm not getting one," she said, turning on her heel. If she couldn't have Quint she didn't want one, and she didn't want to talk about it anymore. It just wasn't fair.

"See you in the morning?" Syd called.

"Yes, thank you," Caroline answered, raising her hand to wave as she walked toward the road. She didn't want to cry in front of them and she could feel it coming on.

If only Mom could come tonight instead of tomorrow, she thought. Mom would know how to say the right thing, even if it wouldn't make Quint hers.

CHAPTER TWENTY

The Pens, Assateague Island, Virginia

Mermaid watched the girl walk away from the pens. Something was different about her today. An aura hung over the girl that felt like winter to the mare, dried out and sad. She shuddered and turned her attention to her son, who was nursing at her side.

The big bay mare shoved him gently, then used strong, square white teeth to pull a clump of dirt from the colt's fur. It had lodged right along the ridge of his back. Next, she licked him softly, grooming his coat until the mud was gone and the fuzzy hair was smooth and clean. Then he danced away, chasing after Orchid's foal.

Mermaid watched her son dodge in and out of the ponies in the pen, weaving past stallions and mares, tagging Orchid's foal with his nose and then spinning away to run in the opposite direction. The two rose on hind legs in a mock stallion fight, then drew apart to race again. At last, the colt shot toward the mare in a burst of speed that ended in a sliding stop. He shoved his head against her side, snorting softly. His play was done.

The sun slowly sank low in the sky. People drifted away from the pens and toward their cars. Night settled over the pens. The frogs were chirping. A lone gull cried out. Mermaid looked over the pens toward Chincoteague Bay. She knew what the morning would bring. She could feel that the number of days in the pen had dwindled away and swim day was almost here.

After Mermaid groomed him, Quint danced away in the pen, chasing after Orchid's foal. Photo by Kathleen Cahall.

Witch Doctor stepped between her and Orchid, rested his head over Mermaid's back momentarily, and then joined her in staring toward the bay. He twisted, rumbled softly at Orchid and Rap the Wind, and then turned his head back to touch Mermaid's nose. It was as if he was saying, "Stay close to me my ladies. Don't get lost in the swim day jumble.

CHAPTER TWENTY-ONE

Chincoteague and Assateague islands, Virginia

The toot of a horn told Caroline her ride had arrived. She stepped onto the porch and into the milky darkness. The sun had not yet risen above the line of trees. She felt her way down the steps, holding onto the porch rail and headed toward the headlights in the driveway.

"Good morning," Syd's mom, Kris, said.

Her stepdad, Jerry, smiled from the driver's seat. "We're glad you could join us."

Caroline smiled. "Me, too. Thanks!"

She slid into the back seat next to Syd. "Did you bring a bathing suit?"

"Yep." She patted her bag. She'd packed snacks, bottled water, and a bathing suit.

They rode in companionable silence, headlights piercing the darkness, heading toward Assateague. A lot of walkers were already on the road, heading for Memorial Park to watch the swim. Caroline was glad she wasn't in that group.

The first rays of early morning sunshine stretched tentatively through the trees as they crossed the bridge onto Assateague Island. There weren't many spectators at the pens, but the cowboys were there, mounted and waiting for the gates to swing open. As soon as the car stopped, Caroline threw her door open and jumped out. Syd was right behind her.

"What's the big hurry?" Kris asked.

Jerry grinned and waved them on. "Do they think we're late?" he asked. "They should know that's not how we roll."

Caroline's stomach hurt when she thought about Quint making the swim, about him being auctioned off as a Buy Back, about him not coming home with her. She practically ran to the pens, but a burly cowboy waved her back when she got too close to the gate.

"You'll have to stay back," he said.

Caroline nodded.

Witch Doctor and his mares and the two colts were standing near the front of the gate. While some of the other horses milled about nervously, this band stood waiting patiently. Watching them, Caroline fell in love all over again. Quint was a part of Mermaid and he would inherit the calm wisdom of Witch Doctor by example. *Why couldn't he go home with her?*

"I wish you could buy him," Syd said quietly. She put her hand on Caroline's arm.

Caroline turned, sucking back the rolling emotions that threatened to engulf her. "Me, too," she said.

"Back now," the burly cowboy said. "We're going to open the gate."

Kris and Jerry were behind them now, and they backed up, joining the scattered group of spectators under the trees by the smaller pen. The gate flew wide and the ponies streamed out.

"Hup, hup, hup," one cowboy called out. Another one snapped a whip in the air. As the ponies left the pen, cowboys on horseback fell into line along the edge of the band, moving them forward, heading for the bay. Caroline knew they would stand on the point of the bay until the water reached slack tide, that time between high and low tide when the water was perfectly still, and then they would swim the short distance to Memorial Park.

After she watched Quint's chestnut tail dance away in the distance, she turned to follow Syd toward the car. She could picture the ponies standing on the point, ready to swim.

"Onward to the beach," Syd said, her voice pumped up with enthusiasm.

She knows how awful I feel inside, Caroline thought, and she forced herself to smile.

As Caroline went on to the beach with her friends, she could picture the ponies standing on the point, ready to swim. Photo by Kathleen Cahall.

That evening when Mom arrived, Caroline fell into her arms. Mom listened while Caroline told her everything all over again, blubbering like a kid who'd just lost her favorite toy. That was the thing with Mom. She understood when her daughter had to get it all out, and afterward, Caroline felt a little less sad.

"Do you want to stay for the auction tomorrow, or do you want to go home?" Mom asked after the tears had subsided.

Caroline thought about it for a few minutes. "I want to go to the auction," she said.

"Are you sure?"

"No, but I have to do it," she said. "I have to be there to show the other Feather Fund kids my support."

The look on Mom's face said it all. There was pride and love and even more love. Seeing it made things seem a little better for Caroline.

CHAPTER TWENTY TWO

The Herds on Assateague Island, Virginia

Mermaid and Orchid stood with their colts and Rap the Wind next to a gate with Witch Doctor on the other side. He'd been shaky and weak after the big swim earlier in the day. The firemen had pulled him out and were giving him fluids through a long tube.

The mare watched intently. She knew her stallion was the oldest one on the island, but she had never seen him shake like that. The firemen were kind. They patted his neck as the man they called Doc Cameron tended to him.

Witch Doctor raised his head and stared. His eyes met Mermaid's and she felt his strength and determination. As she watched, the doctor unhooked the tubes. "Let him rest an hour and then turn him back with his girls," the doctor said. "He'll be fine."

Mermaid turned her attention to her son. He'd stood like a statue, watching Witch Doctor with his momma, curiosity making his ears stand high. Now she lowered her head to touch his nose.

Mermaid nuzzled her colt, then pushed him closer as he turned to nurse. The swim earlier in the day had been a big experience for him, but he'd swum like a champ, treading water in the same way he faced everything in life, with zest and confidence. She didn't want to let him go, but she knew he was ready. She began to slowly lick him along the ridge of his mane. Then she moved her head down to rest lightly on his back, leaning close. Soon it would be time to say goodbye.

Mermaid moved her head down to rest lightly on Quint's back, leaning close. Soon it would be time to say goodbye. Photo by Kathleen Cahall.

CHAPTER TWENTY THREE

Chincoteague Island, Virginia

Caroline's heart raced when the first foal was led into the ring. She recognized Georgia Peach's pretty bay colt.

"Let's start it at $800. How about $800," the auctioneer started.

"$200," someone called.

"Okay, we can start low and work our way up," the auctioneer said. "Two, two, two, we have two… how about three hundred? I have three. Three-fifty?"

The bidding flew. In a matter of moments the foal was sold.

"Only $400?" Caroline stared at her mom. "Unbelievable!" She leaned over in her seat, elbows on knees, heart in her throat. Angry thoughts swept through her head.

"It figures. This is the year the foals are going low, and mine ends up a Buy Back."

"Are you sure they didn't take the tag off today?" Mom said hopefully. "Wasn't someone going to talk to them?"

"Mom! No one can talk to anyone. He has a red tag on him!" She knew she shouldn't have snapped, so Caroline lowered her voice and added, "I checked as soon as we got here."

Mom put her hand on Caroline's shoulder, and they both turned to the ring to see the next foal in, Patchy's beautiful bay pinto filly. She went for $650. Caroline groaned.

Foal after foal was led out, bid on, and sold. The sing-song bidding began to sound like a chant, one that said, "No foal for you… no foal for you." Caroline wiped a hand across her face, hiding tears that threatened.

"Molly's," Lois said when the fifteenth foal came into the ring.

Molly was all business, gaping at the foal inside the ring, the feather she would use to bid jiggling nervously in her hand.

"$500!" Someone called. Molly's feather shot up in the air, and the bidding took off. It didn't stop until the foal

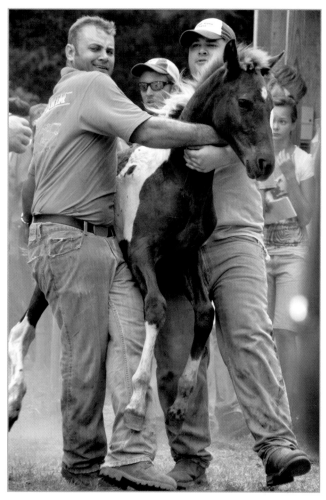

At the auction, Quint came up on his hind legs but the firemen held tight. Photo by Kathleen Cahall.

became Molly's with a resounding $1,500 bid. The tears rolling down Molly's cheeks meshed with her big smile. Everyone hugged her in turns.

"Congratulations, Molly," Caroline said and her words were genuine. It was nice to finally see something good happen on this blue day. If Alana got her colt, too, the one she already called Spartan, that would be the icing on the cake.

Nine foals later, Alana's big bay pinto came into the ring. Alana sat in the row of chairs just in front of Caroline, perched on the edge of her chair, clenching the feather she would raise to bid on her colt.

"Wait for someone else to start the bidding," Lois advised Alana.

Alana leaned forward, nerves making her leg jiggle up and down, up and down.

"Okay, we have $500, do we hear six?" the auctioneer was already calling.

"Six, we have six. Seven, eight, nine, one thousand dollars!" The bidding climbed fast, with numbers called out furiously. Alana jabbed her feather in the air again and again.

"$1,500," the auctioneer called, "sixteen, seventeen, two thousand dollars. I have a bid of two thousand, do I hear $2,500?"

Alana held her feather high. The Feather Fund's limit was $2,500, but someone quickly bid $2,600. Tears rolled down Alana's face.

"Bid it up to $3,000," Lois said, "but no higher." Alana's feather flew into the air, but a split second later the auctioneer was calling, $3,200.

"Use my money," Caroline blurted. I don't need it. Use mine!'

But the bidding came too fast and furious and a moment later Alana's foal was gone, sold to a woman on the other side of the ring for $4,200. Alana sobbed. The foal she'd dreamed of owning for three months was gone.

Tears ran down Caroline's cheeks, and she swatted at them angrily. She knew exactly how Alana felt, and it just wasn't fair. All these years she'd dreamed of coming to Pony Penning and bidding on a foal, and for all those years she thought of it as the best thing that could happen to her. She was wrong.

Lois leaned over to talk to Alana. Her second pick was Mermaid's foal, but since he was out of the question, who was her third pick?

"Shy Anne's foal," Alana answered, but she was clearly still grieving the loss of Leah's foal.

Caroline wanted to run away. "I wish we could leave," she whispered to her mom.

"Do you wanna go?" Mom asked.

"We can't," Caroline said, staring at her lap before looking up. "We all have to be here for Alana, to make sure she gets a foal.

Foal after foal came through the ring until finally the forty-ninth foal was lead in, Shy Anne's bay pinto colt. He had lots of white, something Alana always said she liked. His head was magnificent, with a big white blaze. Caroline crossed her fingers and said a prayer as the bidding took off. Numbers rose so fast it made her head spin, but then, all at once the gavel was coming down. "Sold!" The foal was Alana's, for $1,200.

Alana was getting hugs from everyone. She was sobbing. Caroline knew her feelings must be a mix of grief and exhilaration.

"You will love this foal," Lois said. "Everything happens for a reason."

Alana nodded, tears flowing.

Caroline snorted. She seriously doubted if everything happened for a reason. There was no good reason she had to lose the foal she loved. She'd worked and saved and wished for and wanted Quintilius for so long.

"Do you want to go?" Mom asked.

Caroline shook her head. "No." A steely resolve had set in. "I want to see who buys Quint. Maybe I can keep in touch with the Buy Back buyer."

"Okay," Mom said. The next foal was already in the ring.

The sun rose higher and hotter in the afternoon sky and even though they were under the covered side of the ring, the collected heat made for a sweaty wait.

When Tuleta Star's foal was brought out fifteen foals later Lois turned around to face Caroline. "You are going to be so sad if you don't take a foal home," she said. "Don't you want to bid?"

"No." Caroline's face must have been solid, because Lois didn't push it. She turned back to the ring.

Where is Quint? Caroline wondered. Is he going to be the last one out?

He was next to the last and when he came out, a sudden turn of events unfolded.

"This is a Buy Back," the auctioneer said, "a..." Someone approached the auctioneer. Words were exchanged. The auctioneer laughed, and then he picked the microphone up again. "Folks, this one is NOT going to be a Buy Back. There has been a little confusion. They thought this pinto was a filly. They don't want any more colts on the island, so he has to be sold as a take-home foal." He laughed. "Someone needs to remind these cowboys that you have to look underneath to find out if you've got a colt or a filly."

The crowd rumbled, confused, wondering how could this happen. Never, in all the years of turn back foals had they ever removed a Buy Back tag, but that's what they were doing, cutting the red tag from Quintilius' neck.

"Oh my gosh, Caroline!" Lois had tears rolling down her cheeks. She whispered something to the other board members and then turned back. "If he goes out of your price range, keep bidding. The Feather Fund will lend you the extra money and you can pay them back."

Caroline nodded, bewildered. The first bid had been raised. She drew herself tall in the chair, throwing an arm up, holding a feather high. The bidding whirled… "500, $750, $800, $850… Soon she was bidding $1,000.

Caroline thought of the $1,500 she'd saved, of all the hours mowing and mucking and saving, of all the disappointment and heartbreak and then newfound hope. Could Quintilius be ripped away from her yet again?

"$1,100," someone bid against her. "Do I hear $1,200?"

Quint came up on his hind legs, but the firemen held tight. An answering bid came. "$1,200!"

Caroline's stomach turned over, but her hand flew up. "1,250," she called.

"Hup," the ring spotter called. "$1,250."

The auctioneer slowed. "Okay, now I have $1,250. Do I hear $1,300?"

No answering bid came.

"Twelve hundred fifty going once, going twice, twelve fifty…twelve fifty… sold, for twelve hundred and fifty dollars." The gavel came down.

Caroline leaped to her feet and the tears came then, pouring down her cheeks. Mom was hugging, Lois was hugging, Alana was hugging.

And Quint was hers.

Somehow, Quintilius was coming home.

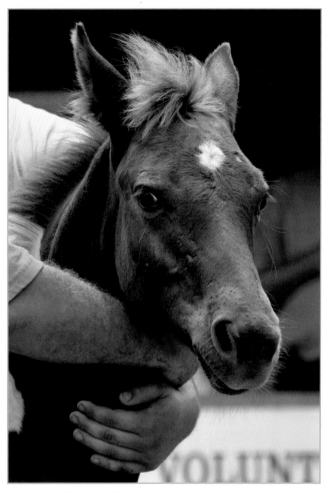

Photo by Kathleen Cahall

UPDATE

Today, two-year-old Quintilius is over 14 hands high. He shares a pasture with Chester on Caroline's family farm in Maryland. Caroline says Quint is a smart gelding who is sometimes ornery like a colt, but he learns fast. She feels maturity is important to a training program, so Caroline has decided to wait until he is three to train him for riding. In the meantime, he has visited schools and libraries with her, introducing kids and adults to the wonderful Chincoteague Pony.

GLOSSARY

Island Terms

ASSATEAGUE ISLAND: Assateague Island is a 33-mile-long island that lies along the coast of Maryland and Virginia. Wild ponies inhabit the island. On the Virginia side (the side that borders Chincoteague Island), Assateague is a wildlife refuge.

CHINCOTEAGUE ISLAND: An island off the coast of Virginia on the East Coast of the United States. The island is seven miles long and one and a half miles wide and is known for its harvest of seafood and the wild pony swim and auction that is held during the last week of July each year. Chincoteague was named by an early Indian tribe; it means "beautiful land across the waters." Chincoteague Island is only four inches above sea level. If not for the barrier island of Assateague, Chincoteague Island would be washed away by the ocean!

CHINCOTEAGUE PONIES: The Assateague Island ponies that live on the Virginia half of Assateague, which are fenced off from the ones on the Maryland side, are called the Chincoteague Ponies. The Chincoteague Volunteer Fire Department owns the Chincoteague Ponies and they have made a concentrated effort to improve the breed by introducing several other breeds into the herds, including Arabians and Mustangs. The resulting pony herds are just as hardy, but more refined. The Chincoteague Ponies now have a registry.

PONY PENNING: Each year the Chincoteague Volunteer Fire Department rounds up all the ponies on the Virginia side of Assateague Island. These saltwater cowboys herd the ponies into the narrowest part of the bay at slack tide and swim them to Chincoteague Island, bringing them ashore at Memorial Park. After a brief rest, the ponies are paraded from Memorial Park to the Chincoteague Fire Department's carnival grounds. They always swim the last Wednesday of July and they are always auctioned off on

Photo by Lois Szymanski.

the last Thursday of July, and then they are returned to the island of Assateague on Friday. This tradition began over 300 years ago as way of controlling herd size, but it became much more. Over the years, it has become a fundraiser for the fire department, as well as a time of great fun and celebration. Pony Penning was made famous in 1947 when Marguerite Henry's children's book, *Misty of Chincoteague*, was published.

Equine Terms

COLT: A boy foal.

FILLY: A girl foal.

FOAL: A baby horse or pony.

FORELOCK: The long hair that grows between the ears of a horse or pony and falls across their forehead.

HERD SIRE: The stallion that leads his band of mares and is the father of the foals they produce.

MANE: The long hair that grows from the neck of a horse or pony from behind the ears to the start of the back.

MARE: A mature female horse or pony.

PONY: A horse that is under fourteen hands in height. Horses are measured from the highest point of the withers (high point of the back) to the ground. Each hand equals four inches.

STALLION: A mature male horse or pony that is still able to father young.

TACK: Equipment specifically for horses. Some of the most used tack includes saddles, bridles, halters, and saddle pads.

TAIL: The long hair that grows from the back of a horse in the same way a puppy or a cat has a tail.

YEARLING: A horse or pony that is one year old.

Chincoteague Pony Colors

BAY: A dark brown horse or pony with a black mane and tail, nose, muzzle, and legs. The black is known as black tips. A bay horse may or may not have white legs or a white marking on the face.

BLACK: Solid black with a black mane and tail.

CHESTNUT: A reddish brown horse or pony with a flaxen, cream-colored, or reddish-colored mane and tail. Chestnut-colored horses are often described as being the color of a new copper penny.

PALOMINO: A golden-colored horse with a cream or flaxen mane and tail.

PINTO: A pinto horse can be white with splotches of color (such as chestnut, bay, palomino, or black) or one of those colors with large spots of white. Chincoteague is known for their many flashy pinto ponies.

ROAN: A solid-colored horse whose coloring is sprinkled with white hairs.

SORREL: A light chestnut.

Pony Markings

STAR: A small white patch on the forehead of the horse between the eyes.

STRIPE: A thin white line down the face of the horse.

BLAZE: A wide strip of white down the face of the horse.

BALD FACE: A wide blaze, extending to or past the eyes.

SNIP: A small strip of color usually on the nose of the horse

Photo by Lois Szymanski.

between the nostrils.

STOCKING: A white leg marking that extends at least to the bottom of the knee or hock, sometimes higher.

SOCK: A white leg marking that extends higher than the fetlock, but not as high as the knee or hock.

BOOT: A white marking that extends over the fetlock and is slightly lower than a sock.

PASTERN: A white marking that extends above the top of the hoof, but stops below the fetlock.

CORONET: A thin line of white around the leg, just above the hoof, around the coronary band. It is usually no more than one inch above the hoof.